Archaeology and
Brita...

Paul Spoerry

1993

RESCUE, *The British Archaeological Trust*

Acknowledgements

This volume was completed with the help of several members of the RESCUE Committee. Mike Daniels, Pete Hinton, Jean Mellor, Jude Plouviez and Hedley Swain all provided advice and comment. Particular thanks must be extended to Tony Scrase who not only gave expert comment on an early draft, but also provided additional information that helped greatly in filling a number of gaps, and demystifying tortuous legal text. John Wood also provided extra information concerning the interface between archaeological concerns and countryside legislation. Publication has, as ever, been expertly organised by Hedley Swain.

Finally, thanks must go to my wife Pam without whose continuing support and help with text input and layout, this document would never have been completed.

P.S.S., February 1993

1993

ISBN 9037 89-16-7

Published by RESCUE, the British Archaeological Trust.

Further copies available from:
RESCUE
15 Bull Plain,
Hertford,
Herts SG14 1DX

Contents

Introduction

This short volume has been produced to provide a much-needed overall picture of the various pieces of legislation and government guidance that have some bearing on archaeology in the United Kingdom. Such documents are disparate in nature, often difficult to obtain and regularly consist of dozens of pages of text with only a single sentence or paragraph that is of relevance to archaeology. All of us who are active in one aspect or other of the 'broad church' of professional archaeology occasionally need some of this information. Many of us have tried to find such facts, and have waded despairingly through pages of legal language and notes concerning the proper procedures for the laying of sewers or the construction of lock-up garages! It is hoped that this volume will render such chores obsolete for most of us who only require broad guidelines to the existing legal and procedural framework. Others who wish more detail may also find this document useful in targeting 'where to go' for the definitive statement. The paragraph headings below should be self-explanatory and a full list of the source documents is included at the end of the volume. Wherever possible attempts have been made to keep all sections up-to-date at the time of final editing and printing. Of course, a booklet as wide ranging as this one, in terms of the documents discussed and cited, may well become out-dated in some areas quite quickly. If this is due to the introduction of new and more comprehensive legislation, then this author, for one, will not mind. In the absence of any such new introductions any omissions or mistakes remain the author's responsibility and comments on such are of course welcome (through the RESCUE Office).

Part 1 Areas of Statutory Protection

Ancient Monuments Legislation

United Kingdom legislation directly relating to archaeology in general, or rescue archaeology in particular, is not common. The only act that addresses archaeological matters as a *raison d'etre* is the *Ancient Monuments and Archaeological Areas Act 1979*, and its amendments in the *National Heritage Act 1983.* The 1979 act deals specifically with Scheduled Ancient Monuments and designated Areas of Archaeological Importance (AAI's). There are currently about 13,000 of the former in England, and the English Heritage Monuments Protection Programme, which aims to evaluate all known archaeological remains in England, is expected to make substantial additions to this number over the next few years. There are presently 2,600 Scheduled Ancient Monuments in Wales, Scotland has 4,500, whilst there are almost 1,000 in Northern Ireland. As'scheduled monument consent', which enables potentially destructive activities to take place, has regularly been granted, in some cases resulting in major destruction, it must be assumed that the actual purpose of scheduling is not necessarily to preserve in perpetuity, but to provide a check or breathing space so that proper consideration can be given if a real threat becomes apparent. According to the recent government white paper 'This Common Inheritance'(1990) which outlines government thinking on many facets of the 'environment debate' across the whole of the UK, an assessment programme is underway which is intended to ascertain whether the protection provided under the 1979 Act is both relevant and adequate.

In practice most proposals for the scheduling of monuments originate with English Heritage, Cadw, the Northern Ireland Office of the DoE or Historic Scotland, although it is theoretically the relevant Secretary of State's duty to maintain the schedule. A Scheduled Ancient Monument can be almost any structure of human construction or area of known archaeological deposits. Exceptions are churches in ecclesiastical use, marine structures already protected under the *Protection of Wrecks Act 1973*, and occupied dwellings. Before scheduling goes ahead the owner(s) and occupiers(s) are usually approached with the proposal and allowed to make comments for referral to the Ancient Monuments Board. When necessary a monument can be scheduled without prior consultation, but this only occurs in 'emergencies' to prevent imminent destruction. Once a monument is scheduled, then scheduled monument consent is required before any works are carried out that would have the effect of demolishing, destroying, damaging, removing, repairing, altering, adding to, flooding or covering up the monument. Exceptions do, however, exist and these are outlined in a separate document *The Ancient Monuments (Class Consents) Order 1981*. This lists six 'class consents', defining occasions when automatic 'scheduled monument consent' is granted. These are:

Class I. Agricultural, horticultural or forestry works of the same kind that has been executed in that field or location for the five years up to 9th October 1981, but not including subsoiling, drainage works, the planting or uprooting of trees, hedges, shrubs or any other works likely to disturb the soil below the maximum depth affected by normal ploughing.

Class II. Works more than 10m below ground by the NCB or its licencees.

Class III. Certain routine operations by the British Waterways Board.

Class IV. Works for the repair or maintenance of machinery, where they will not materially alter the monument.

Class V. Works essential for health or public safety.

Class VI. Works by English Heritage.

Where works that will adversely affect the scheduled monument and which do not come under one of the six 'class consents' are proposed, separate consent applications may have to be submitted for each phase of the work, e.g. archaeological evaluation, preservation by record (usually excavation) and the works themselves. Funding for the necessary archaeological work is in theory provided by the developer, with assistance from one of the national bodies only where absolutely necessary.

Any person found guilty of breaching scheduled monument consent can be fined up to £5,000 on summary conviction in a Magistrates Court, or an unlimited sum on indictment by a Crown Court. The further offence of damaging a Scheduled Ancient Monument without a lawful excuse can also result in a prison sentence of up to six months on summary conviction, and up to two years on indictment. Where a case of damage to a Scheduled Ancient Monument is taken seriously by a Crown Court, large fines can thus result. One case in 1991 resulted in a £75,000 fine being imposed on a company for damage to a Scheduled Ancient Monument in Southwark, London, although this was reduced on appeal. Such substantial penalties are welcome, but they are by no means the norm. A further concern is the lack of clarification regarding the exact relationship of these Scheduled Ancient Monument offences, in relation to each other, and to other offences involving the use of metal detectors on, and the removal of objects from, designated sites.

Overall the 1979 legislation usually provides adequate protection for that portion of the nation's archaeology deemed by the 'national heritage bodies' to be important enough to be worth scheduling. In cases where sites are considered for scheduling after planning permission has been granted, however, it is possible that scheduling may not in fact go ahead, due to the relevant national heritage body fearing substantial compensation. This is by no means far-fetched and has been cited by some as a major cause in the escalation of the Rose Theatre crisis in 1989. It is an unavoidable consequence of the nature of archaeological evidence that the archaeological potential of some sites will only become fully apparent after planning permission has been given and an evaluation has been executed, usually in order to satisfy a 'condition' on the permission. It would be reassuring if in such cases the Government and its agencies could be counted upon to support the scheduling recommendation, however, it is apparent that this is not always the case.

In a comparison of ancient monuments and historic buildings legislation published in Rescue News in 1989 (RN49, 4), Martin Scott identified differences in the two sets of provisions which he believed were to the detriment of the level of protection afforded to the former. He suggested that ancient monuments legislation should be updated along lines comparable to that for historic buildings. The specific areas of concern identified by Scott were the need to give local authorities some power in enforcing repairs to, and compulsory purchase of, scheduled monuments, and also the need to allow class consents to be repealed, when the consent is undoubtedly resulting in damage to the monument. This latter specifically relates to cases where ploughing of a monument is being allowed to continue, purely because the owner claims the site was previously ploughed between October 1976 and October 1981, a justification under Class I of the 1981 'Class Consents Order'. No directly comparable situation exists relating to damage to the standing structure of an historic building, however, it cannot be satisfactory that an instance where part of a site is scheduled and a related structure listed could see continued destruction of the buried archaeology, with full protection only being afforded to the standing building. Also if one area of a monument were both Listed and Scheduled, it is the latter, weaker, power that takes precedence, thus preventing the local authority from protecting the site through the extended powers of 'repairs enforcement' and 'compulsory purchase'. One final area where new ancient monuments legislation could benefit from being modelled on that for standing buildings is in the removal of 'ignorance' as a defence for cases involving alleged damage to Scheduled Ancient Monuments.

In 1991 proposals for changes to the 1979 Ancient Monuments Act were circulated to County Archaeologists. These proposals cover seven areas and include a widening of the scope of the definition of 'damage' to Scheduled Ancient Monuments and, more importantly, the possibility of removal of 'ignorance' as a defence in cases involving 'damage'. The proposals also suggest legislative changes whereby local authorities or the national heritage body would have the power to carry out urgent repairs to an ancient monument, but there would be no provision to then charge the owner as is the case with listed buildings legislation *(Planning (Listed Buildings and Conservation Areas) Act 1990)*. These proposals, if implemented as law, would cover most of the inadequacies cited by Scott (above and 1989), but they do not, however, address problems relating to potential compensation claims, nor do they include provision for the removal of class consents which result in continuing destruction of the site.

Areas of Archaeological Importance

There are at present only five designated AAIs, all of them in England. They are the historic cores of the towns of Canterbury, Chester, Exeter, Hereford and York. Although, in 1987 the House of Commons Environment Committee recommended that the Secretary of State initiate consultations with local authorities with a view to establishing further AAIs, English Heritage has since then (15/11/88) made it clear that it does not intend recommending the designation of any more AAIs. Thus all rural areas, and the great majority of Britain's historic towns, are not covered by this part of the 1979 Act.

Within an AAI potential developers are required to:

"give six weeks' notice to the relevant planning authority of all proposals to disturb the ground, tip on it or flood it. The investigating authority for the area (nominated by the Secretary of State) then has the power to enter the site and, if necessary, to excavate it for up to four and a half months before development may proceed. The Act makes no financial provisions for the costs of administering the scheme" (*PPG16*, Annex 3, 19, Nov 1990).

Thus a 'breathing space' is afforded to threatened archaeology within AAIs, but the actual progress of a planning application and the funding of any resultant archaeological works is theoretically dealt with in exactly the same way as with similar applications relating to sites elsewhere. There is, of course, the expectation that the academic potential of archaeological remains within AAIs will be high and any planning decisions will take account of this. The legislation regarding AAIs applies to all proposals to disturb the ground and therefore includes work by statutory undertakers such as the water and electricity companies, which does not usually require planning consent, but the Act includes no financial provision for archaeological work from local or central government, or from the prospective agents of destruction. It is this failing that led to the 1989 crisis on the Queen's Hotel site in York: for a long time there had been simply no money to excavate this very important site. It is probable that the AAIs scheme, as it stands, is not popular with government. Whether this is because the legislation is perceived to be unworkable in its present form, there being no mandatory financial provision for any necessary archaeological recording, or whether it is purely a dislike of real development restrictions on behalf of government, is open to debate. It is believed by some that as implementation of PPG16 becomes accepted, the AAI legislation will be rendered more and more irrelevant. Nevertheless there are some aspects which may still have useful application.

All archaeological deposits in the UK which are not part of a Scheduled Ancient Monument or within an AAI are unprotected by the 1979 Act. Such remains form the larger part of the nation's archaeological heritage and their protection is reliant on the application of specific aspects of planning law, government guidance and the recommendations of independent bodies. This complex array of documentation, and the theoretical pathways through it are discussed in Part Two.

Portable Antiquities Legislation

Portable antiquities are at present only covered by the law on treasure trove and numerous laws relating to property. Treasure trove law derives from royal prerogative powers, the origins of which can be traced back to the medieval period. A 1987 Law Commission paper on the reform of treasure trove law describes the basis of existing legislation as:

"if articles of gold or silver in coin, bullion or plate have been concealed in the ground or other hiding place with a view to later repossession by an owner who can no longer be traced, such treasure when subsequently unearthed belongs to the crown" (Law Commission, Sept. 1987).

The problems with this legislation are many, but the major issues are perhaps that: firstly, objects that have been lost, or intentionally abandoned (such as grave goods), are not classed as treasure trove and thus become the property of the landowner (or sometimes the finder). Secondly, only some classes of artefact (those with high gold or silver content) can become treasure trove, which obviously does not include the overwhelming majority of archaeological material. Thus groups of artefacts of different material, but found together, are treated differently. Furthermore objects with partial gold or silver content require scientific analysis and/or informed debate to determine their status under the law. There are a number of other problems, but one particular aspect of great concern is the fact that as long as many portable artefacts remain outside the legal classification (and thus will usually remain the property of the landowner or finder) then there is reason enough for greedy and unscrupulous individuals to remove such objects from known, but unclassified archaeological sites. Recent attempts to introduce new legislation to replace that for treasure trove have as yet proved unsuccessful (e.g. a bill was presented in December 1990, but not passed).

In Northern Ireland the *Ancient Monuments (Northern Ireland) Act 1925* affords greater protection to archaeological objects, these being defined as:

"any manufactured or unmanufactured chattel which by reason of its archaeological or historic interest has a value substantially greater than its intrinsic value or the value of the composition materials" (*ibid.*).

Finds of this category must be reported to the Ancient Monuments Advisory Council within fourteen days, with failure to do so, or fraud, resulting in a fine or imprisonment. Because of the broad range of the descriptive terms, most portable archaeological material is protected under this particular law. It is self-evident therefore that the law in Northern Ireland is much more well-disposed towards the need to protect portable antiquities than the law in the rest of the United Kingdom.

International trade in portable antiquities is theoretically subject to a UNESCO convention (1970). This requires states party to the convention to prevent the trade in cultural property involving individuals and bodies within their own jurisdiction, as well as charging all party states to provide national services responsible for the protection of its own cultural heritage. There is also a statement requiring party states to endeavour to educate their populace in both the value of cultural property, and the nature of threats to the cultural heritage. Such grand statements are undeniably welcome, however, the effectiveness of the convention in preventing illicit antiquities trading has to be in doubt. Certainly there is a large international market for antiquities at all levels of value (cultural and monetary), and, even ignoring clandestine transactions, by no means all of the trading that occurs legally and openly would be acceptable if the convention were strictly applied. For many years the United States, a signatory of the convention, was perhaps the largest market for illicit antiquities trading in the world. In the last few years the US Government has, however, made greater efforts to stamp out such illegal activities and it is probably now in Britain that the greatest volume of transactions occurs. The British Government has never ratified the UNESCO convention (Henig 1986), apparently claiming that our own legislation is good enough on its own! This is undoubtedly not the case as we do not have any modern dedicated portable antiquities legislation in this country. It may well be that the British Government's real concern is for the effect that strict adherence to the convention would have on the London auction houses and the balance of trade figures.

There have unfortunately been many recent examples illustrating how bad the protection afforded to British antiquities really is. One of the more notorious examples is the case of the Icklingham Bronzes (Plouviez 1989). These were apparently looted from a Scheduled Ancient Monument by thieves using metal detectors. This crime occurred at night, sometime in 1982, and since then the only evidence for the material is rumour and fifteen photographs, taken at various times whilst the objects travelled between dealers and countries. Despite the efforts of the landowner, RESCUE and others, the Office of Arts and Libraries refused to take any action to recover the objects once they resurfaced in the USA. This led to a Rescue statement concluding that;

"in practice, it is impossible for this government to recover heritage items which have been illegally removed to another country regardless of their importance or the circumstances involved" (reprinted in RN49, 2).

Whether this situation would be radically altered if Britain were to sign the UNESCO convention is open to question. It would certainly not make matters worse, but the answer may in fact lie with proper internal legislation, coupled with a will to see such an act work. *The Ancient Monuments (Northern Ireland) Act 1925* is a good basis to work from, as is the failed 1990 treasure trove reform bill. Until such moves are made the most effective way of legislating against such trade may be to attempt to stop it at source, with strict application of existing legislation as used by the police in Norfolk and Suffolk (Plouviez 1989, RN49). If more prosecutions can be brought on individuals 'going equipped to steal' (carrying a metal detector around the countryside at 2am) or of 'theft' (removing objects from land without the owner's permission), then valuable steps are surely being taken.

Recently (Feb 1992) in the House of Lords, Lord Kennet asked for an explanation of the reasons why the government has not ratified the 1970 UNESCO convention. The reply (Viscount Astor) was that ratification would "expose us to formidable bureaucratic problems including differences of interpretation of the meaning of cultural goods." (Reported in *British Archaeological News* Volume 7 No.2, March 1992). Subsequently a strongly worded statement was made by Lord Renfrew, which indicated the extent of illicit antiquities trading in the United Kingdom. This also produced a reply from Viscount Astor which stated he was "not aware that there is a large trade in smuggled goods in this country", and again re-stated the government's belief that "we have our own laws which we feel achieve many of the same objectives as the convention" (*op cit*). It is therefore apparent that official line in regard of this subject has not changed since Martin Henig made his comments in 1986 (see above).

Listed Buildings Legislation

The *Planning (Listed Buildings and Conservation Areas) Act 1990* consolidated many measures that had come into being over the previous nineteen years, starting with the *Town and Country Planning Act 1971* and including a major reworking of this in 1988. The most recent addition to the relevant legislation is the *Planning and Compensation Act 1991*, which has in particular, made changes in the penalties that can be imposed for breaches of the 1990 legislation. Some aspects of listed buildings legislation, and how it compares to that for ancient monuments, have already been discussed. A brief overview of the main points is given here.

Officially the Secretary of State for the Environment is compiler of the list in England. A listed building is one recognised by government as being of special architectural or historic interest. The listing relates to the building itself, to objects or structures fixed to the building, and to pre-1948 objects or structures within the curtilage of the building. In actuality many objects that cannot be classified as buildings are listed, such as post-boxes, steps or gates. Listing is made at three levels of importance, in ascending order, Grade II, Grade II* and Grade I. Procedures exist whereby local authorities (and English Heritage in London) have the power temporarily to list a building, usually when under threat, through use of a Building Preservation Notice. This then gives six months' protection whilst a long term decision is made. Alternatively a reasonably quick 'spot listing' may be undertaken, usually when the threat is not immediate, but still evident. Once listed, much tighter controls on development and alterations to the building can be exerted by the planning authority. Central to these controls is the need to acquire Listed Building Consent before undertaking any alterations which; "affect its character as a building of architectural or special interest". Planning permission will still be needed if the proposed works would normally require it. In many instances consent needs to be acquired for internal alterations, as well as for more obvious external ones. The decision as to whether consent is granted rests with the relevant planning authority for all listed buildings, although in the case of Grade II* and Grade I structures, consultation with the national heritage body must be sought, although the resulting advice can still be ignored. In cases where the LPA (Local Planning Authority) intends to allow demolition, the Secretary of State can be called in to deal with the matter personally.

If consent is not granted the developer used to be eligible for compensation in some cases. This does not now apply, except for applications which were lodged before the sixteenth of November 1991. If Listed Building Consent is ignored, or not requested, the local planning authority can issue a Listed Building Enforcement Notice. This may require that the building be returned to its former state, or that it be improved or altered so that the damage is lessened. In cases where the enforcement notice is upheld, and the necessary works are not executed, then prosecution or 'default action' may result. This latter allows the planning authority to enter and carry out the necessary works, and then recover the costs from the owner. This power is subject to appeal, however, and appears to be rarely used. Fines and imprisonment for actions damaging historic buildings can be quite substantial and some recent cases have seen the level of punishment increase. Local planning authorities are also able to serve an Urgent Repairs Notice on the owner of a dilapidated unoccupied listed building. The notice gives the owner seven days' notice of works that the planning authority will carry out to preserve the building. The cost of the works can be recovered from the owner, who can appeal against the amount to the Secretary of State. A listed building that has not been repaired in line with a repairs notice may be compulsorily purchased by the local planning authority or by the national heritage body. The owner is, however, entitled to compensation, potentially of a very large size. Local authorities also have the power of compulsory purchase in cases where the owner of a listed building allows it to fall into disrepair in order to redevelop the site. The price paid for the property in such cases may be drastically reduced.

It is apparent that historic buildings legislation is very comprehensive in its powers of preservation and regulation, with respect to listed structures. Listing is thus an important statement of intent to preserve on behalf of Government and its agencies. The basic criteria by which buildings are considered for listing are outlined in Appendix 1 of *DoE Circular 8/87 Historic Buildings and Conservation Areas - Policy and Procedures*. The criteria of selection cover four groups of structures:-

> All buildings built before 1700 which survive in anything like their original condition are listed.
>
> Most buildings of 1700-1840 are listed, though selection is necessary.
>
> Between 1840 and 1914 only buildings of definite quality and character are listed, and the selection is designed to include the principal works of the principal architects.
>
> Between 1914 and 1939, selected buildings of high quality are listed.

Added to this, post-1939 buildings can be listed.

In choosing buildings particular attention is paid to:-

> Special value within certain types, either for architectural or planning reasons, or as illustrating social and economic history (for instance industrial buildings, railway stations, schools, hospitals, theatres, town halls, markets, exchanges, almshouses, prisons, lock-ups, mills).
>
> Technological innovation or virtuosity (for instance cast-iron, pre-fabrication or early use of concrete).
>
> Association with well-known characters or events.
>
> Group value, especially as examples of town planning (for instance, squares, terraces or model villages).

Further, more detailed, qualifying criteria are provided for interwar buildings.

With regard to the grading of listed structures, Appendix 1 of *Circular 8/87* states the following.

The buildings are classified in grades to show their relative importance as follows:-

Grade I These are buildings of exceptional interest (only about 2% of listed buildings so far are in this grade).

Grade II* These are particularly important buildings of more than special interest (4% of listed buildings).

Grade II These are buildings of special interest, which warrant every effort being made to preserve them.

Conservation Areas

The second half of the 1990 Act concerns Conservation Areas. These can be designated by local authorities, and are created to preserve the character and appearance of areas which have been deemed to be of special architectural or historic interest (the latter criterion can be applied to both buried remains and earthworks). In this way legislation regarding conservation areas relates, not just to buildings, listed or otherwise, but to the arrangement and spacing of structures and their relationship to other elements such as parkland, squares etc. Very detailed and specific rules are provided relating to what type of development can take place within conservation areas; this being 'permitted development'. Besides these rules Conservation Area Consent is required before any building within a conservation area, listed or not, is demolished. Furthermore, within conservation areas, planning permission may be subject to special consultation procedures and the local planning authority must decide whether any works or developments will adversely affect the character and appearance of the area. Conservation Area Consent must be granted for works and Urgent Repairs Notices can be served in a manner similar to that described for Listed Buildings, but within conservation areas the legislation can be applied to any structure. As with Listed Buildings, Conservation Areas are discussed in *DoE Circular 8/87*. Much additional guidance on the designation of Conservation Areas is provided. This includes the identification of conflict between Conservation Area and Simplified Planning Zone Status, and the resultant need to keep such designations separate, plus a more general indication of the likely diverse nature of Conservation Areas and the need to see them as a *planning control*, rather than a *planning prevention measure*. This last point is fundamental to the Government's belief that Conservation Area designations and the listing process should not prevent local economic prosperity, but instead moderate development in a positive fashion.

DoE Circular 8/87 also identifies the need to view Conservation Area designation in the context of any relevant development plan policy. More recent legislation has been more explicit in identifying comprehensive development plans as a firm basis by which local planning decisions can be made in a systematic manner.

The Planning (Listed Buildings and Conservation Areas) Regulations 1990 (Statutory Instrument 1519), provide information additional to that found in *DoE circular 8/87*, regarding listing and the designation of Conservation Areas. This document is particularly concerned with the mechanics of both processes and it includes examples of the notices to be served when either process is set in motion.

Other Planning Legislation and Archaeology

Besides the *Planning (Listed Buildings and Conservation Areas) Act 1990* and associated documents, there are other pieces of planning legislation which regulate the preservation (or otherwise) of archaeological material.

The Town and Country Planning Act 1990 and The Planning and Compensation Act 1991

The former of these two pieces of legislation provides the basis of planning law in this country. The whole process of seeking planning permission, and descriptions of what is not permitted, for whatever reason, is detailed. Most of this is not of direct relevance here, although it should be borne in mind that this is the framework around which all further planning legislation and control methodologies operate.

The Planning and Compensation Act 1991 seeks to clarify various points outlined in the 1990 Act and introduces new procedures as regards compensation and land acquisition, enforcement actions and development plans. The latter is of particular interest to those concerned with the protection of the 'cultural heritage'.

The new legislation heightens the status of development plans by explicitly stating that, where determinations are being made under planning legislation, "regard is to be had to the development plan and the determination shall be in accordance with the plan unless material considerations indicate otherwise". Thus the *onus* is on the relevant archaeological bodies and officers to make sure that due consideration is given to archaeology and historic buildings and structures within the development plan for each area. In doing so provision is then made for the protection of the 'cultural heritage' in a structured manner, relating directly to localised concerns and preservation and research objectives. Such procedures, where carried out properly, should go a long way towards preventing the protection of the material remains of the past remaining a 'knee-jerk' response to development-initiated crises. As regards the Development Plan system, the 1991 Act outlines how such documents, whether concerned with Unitary Development Plans, Structure Plans or Local Plans, should include policies in respect of -

i) the conservation of the natural beauty and amenity of the land;
ii) the improvement of the physical environment, and
iii) the management of traffic.

Although archaeology or 'the cultural resource' are not individually mentioned it is not difficult to see such considerations introduced under points i), or ii), where appropriate.

The 1991 Act specifically deals with Listed Buildings, with regard to offences under the existing legislation and the penalties that can be imposed for such offences. The maximum fine for breaches of listed building controls and listed building enforcement is increased to £20,000. This is four times the statutory maximum and shows particular concern for listed buildings (and other planning) offences. Furthermore, magistrates will now have to consider financial benefits accruing, or likely to accrue, as a result of the offence when determining the level of penalty to be imposed. The alternative to a fine (or alongside one) is imprisonment for up to two years.

Environmental Effects (Statutory Instrument 1199)

Statutory Instrument 1199, the *Town and Country Planning (Assessment of Environmental Effects) Regulations 1988* is a piece of legislation outlining cases when a development requires an environmental impact statement as an accompaniment to the application for planning permission. Such statements are required for some large industrial and some agricultural activities and developments that are likely to have an identifiable impact on the local and general environment. Two schedules of the relevant developments are given. Schedule 1 lists developments such as the building of thermal power stations, the disposal of radioactive waste, the extraction of asbestos, building special roads and aerodromes etc. that may cause major environmental effects, but are generally seen as necessary in the eyes of government. Schedule 2 lists many more developments, mostly industrial, but some agricultural or leisure-based, all of which may have some environmental effects, but which are in general not absolutely necessary in any particular instance. A proposal for a development under Schedule 1 requires an Environmental Statement, which identifies the likely environmental impact of the proposed development. Under Schedule 2 the decision as to whether an Environmental Statement is needed rests with the local planning authority (LPA). Once provided, the Environmental Statement is then used as part of the basis by which the Planning Authority and/or Secretary of State decide whether planning permission should be given. If the decision is that the development would be likely, "to have significant effects on the environment by virtue of factors such as its nature, size or location" (para. 2, 3), then the recommendation may be that planning permission is refused, or is only given subject to alterations to the specification of the development. Where the development will result in damage to known archaeological sites, or will damage natural landscapes along with their historical/archaeological component, it is hoped that specialist archaeological advice is sought in compiling the impact assessment. This would then detail the likely effects and damage, and provide a scheme which would minimise such effects, or mitigate the loss through record. This process relies on the relevant archaeological curator, or the planning authority making clear to the developer the necessity of the inclusion of archaeological considerations in the assessment. Failing this, it requires the planning authority to identify when such clauses are absent in an assessment, and then refuse permission if necessary, with the relevant explanation. It is therefore apparent that it is not the law itself, but its application by planning officers, that is the major factor in dictating whether archaeological matters are given due consideration in environmental assessments. This situation is not helped by the wording of the regulations. Although 'cultural heritage' is identified as an area for impact considerations, nowhere in the Statutory Instrument is it explicitly stated that this includes the buried historic environment.

The Environmental Effects Regulations are supplemented by the DoE and Welsh Office Joint Circular 15/88 (WO 23/88) which, in particular, provides further advice as to which Schedule 2 projects will be affected by the need to provide an Environmental Statement (paras 18-33). The Secretary of State's view, as stated in this document, is that three main types of cases will be involved. These are:-

1. Major projects which are of more than local importance.

2. Smaller-scale projects in particularly sensitive locations, e.g. National Parks, SSSIs, AONBs, National Nature Reserves and areas or monuments of major archaeological importance.

3. Projects with unusually complex and potentially adverse environmental effects where expert advice would be relevant and desirable.

The 'General Development Order'

The Town and Country Planning General Development Order 1988 (GDO) is designed to permit certain forms of development without express planning permission under the 1990 Act. In many cases permission is only given subject to extensive qualifications and restrictions. A few restrictions relate to'sites of archaeological interest', which are defined as;

"...land which is included in the schedule of monuments compiled by the Secretary of State under section 1 of the Ancient Monuments and Archaeological Areas Act 1979, or is within an area of land which is designated as an area of archaeological importance under section 33 of that Act, or which is within a site registered in any record kept by a county council and known as the County Sites and Monuments Record."

For example mineral extraction that would otherwise proceed under the GDO may be halted until planning permission is gained if damage to a 'site of archaeological interest' may result. Although few other specifically defined situations exist where the powers of the GDO are blocked for archaeological reasons, it is certainly significant that a legal definition of a 'site of archaeological interest' is in existence. It is, however, unfortunate that such explicit archaeologically-derived restrictions do not also extend to developments such as road construction by central and local government, or afforestation.

Archaeology and Legislation in the Countryside

Some archaeological sites and landscapes are afforded a degree of protection through countryside legislation.

The Countryside Act 1968 is part of the legislation that empowers the Countryside Commission. It enables National Parks to provide educational and tourist facilities for 'objects of architectural, archaeological or historical interest' within their areas and gives responsibilities to government and public bodies to take account of countryside matters in all aspects of their work.

The Wildlife and Countryside Act 1981 also gives protection to historic components of the landscape through the use of section 39 management agreements to conserve and enhance landscape 'amenity'.

The Agriculture Act 1986 includes Environmentally Sensitive Areas (ESA) legislation, which provides some protection for historic features in traditional landscapes. The scheme is due to be reviewed this year, but it has already contributed to archaeological conservation. Within ESA's farmers are offered management agreements all of which include a requirement to manage positively "such key environmental features as walls, field barns, ditches and dykes."

The Countryside Commission and The Countryside Council for Wales

Recent policy documents produced by these bodies do not consider archaeological issues specifically. The Countryside Commission's 1991 Policy Document *An Agenda for the Countryside* does however include the statement : "The beauty of the countryside - which includes its wildlife and its cultural identity - is enhanced by diversity. Geology and landform, natural and semi-natural vegetation, local building materials and styles, farming practices, a sense of place, and local traditions all create a precious variety that should be maintained" (Countryside Commission 1991). As previously described the Countryside Commission is responsible for watching over England's national parks on the government's behalf under *The Countryside Act 1968*. The Countryside Commission has in recent years specifically identified the importance of the archaeological and historical components of landscapes within designated National Parks. In 1987 a publication entitled *The National Park Authority* stated that national parks "contain our most beautiful areas of countryside. They are important for the diversity of their landscapes and wildlife and for their historic settlements and archaeological remains" (Countryside Commission 1987). This same document explained the roles of the National Parks Authorities (NPAs) which include the provision of "grants and technical advice to owners of historic buildings to aid in restoration; they also designate conservation areas, carry out town improvement schemes and remove eyesores. A few NPAs own or manage ancient monuments, working with English Heritage, or Cadw in Wales. They carry out studies to protect field monuments and to conserve or restore relics of industrial history and make them accessible and understandable by visitors" (*op. cit.*).

In March 1991 the National Parks Review Committee published a report entitled '*Fit for the Future.*' It included the following recommendations;

"a comprehensive and comparative archaeological database for each national park should be developed jointly by the various recording agencies. Archaeological research should be given a higher priority, and national park authorities should strengthen their links with academic institutions.

Archaeological Conservation should be linked with our proposed farm plans, together with an increased use of Guardianship Agreements and Rural Conservation Areas. Rural Areas of Archaeological Importance and Landscape Conservation Orders should be made available as reserve powers.

There should be more effective and integrated archaeological legislation, particularly in relation to the protection and scheduling of Ancient Monuments" (Countryside Commission 1991, 24).

The indications are therefore that the Countryside Commission would welcome more wide-ranging and explicit archaeological legislation, and that significant efforts to protect and manage archaeological remains within designated areas should be expected in the future. This will be further helped by another recommendation which suggested that the National Park Authorities should all review their expertise in archaeology, historic buildings and interpretation.

The Countryside Stewardship Scheme

The Countryside Commission has recently announced a new national countryside initiative designed to enhance and re-create valued English landscapes and habitats. 'Countryside Stewardship', as it is known, will in the first instance concentrate on five wide-ranging categories of landscapes and habitats; chalk and limestone grassland, heathland, waterside landscapes, coastal land and uplands. The aims of the scheme are to make incentives available to landowners and managers to establish management practices that enhance or restore aspects of these landscape and habitat types. The historic dimension of the environment is specifically identified as a matter for consideration. Qualifying initiatives will receive awards, with particular interest being expressed in examples which improve opportunities for people to visit, appreciate and enjoy the landscapes in their restored form.

The New Nature Conservation Agencies and Archaeology

During the debate on the Committee stage of the Countryside Bill in the House of Lords in 1990 some amendments drafted by the CBA Countryside Committee were tabled, which were designed to ensure that the new nature conservation agencies took proper account of the archaeological heritage in their work. These were withdrawn following an undertaking by Government to incorporate this principle in a binding Statement of Intent. This document was agreed by all parties involved and came into effect on 1st April 1991. It was issued jointly by the NCC, English Heritage, Cadw and Historic Scotland, and identifies the need for all land management initiatives designed to provide for better nature conservation to take into account the effect of such developments on the archaeological component of the landscape, and vice versa. Implementation of this joint statement now falls to the 'successor Councils', since the replacement of the NCC by English Nature, the NCC for Scotland and the Countryside Council for Wales.

In the *Joint Statement,* the signatory bodies have agreed:

1. To exchange information about all nature conservation and archaeological sites, including SSSIs, National Nature Reserves and Scheduled Ancient Monuments, and to agree the management of those sites where mutual interest is involved.
2. To discuss with local authority archaeologists and in Scotland Regional Archaeological Trusts ways of ensuring that the needs of other archaeological sites are taken into account when land is being managed for nature conservation.
3. To collaborate on issues of mutual interest and to foster an

understanding of the interdependence of nature conservation and archaeology.
(Nature Conservancy Council April 1991).

It is therefore apparent that recent developments have formalised relationships between archaeological and nature conservation bodies, and some commonality in approach has been established. There is still, however, a pressing need for proper legislation to deal with archaeological preservation and management in rural areas, as identified by the Countryside Commission in their March 1991 paper. Individual management agreements for archaeological landscapes within specially designated areas, be they national parks, AONBs, ESA, only provide a partial solution to the problems of caring for the archaeological heritage in rural areas.

Archaeology and Forestry

Under the Forestry Act 1967 the Forestry Commission may not compulsorily purchase land which is the site of an Ancient Monument or other object of archaeological interest. This unequivocal statement with regard to new acquisitions by the Forestry Commission does not, however, extend protection in any way to the vast numbers of archaeological sites on land currently in their ownership. The Commission's Policy Paper No. 1 does offer a better perspective and states:

"it will take account of good land use... and the use of management systems which protect and enhance the environment and safeguard sites important for the conservation of nature and for archaeology"

This is representative of a greatly increased awareness of the needs of archaeology, on behalf of the Commission, which has resulted in new afforestation initiatives, such as the Woodland Grant Scheme (1988), arriving complete with additional literature explaining the requirements of archaeology and identifying the minimum standards expected of all applicants to the scheme. A leaflet produced for the example above stated that

"It is Forestry Commission policy that planting should not damage sites which archaeologists regard as important."

Such statements are laudable, however, as Ian Shepherd rightly pointed out in his 1989 paper in the CSA publication *Our Vanishing Heritage*, (Proudfoot 1989) the great problem that archaeologists have in the heavily afforested regions, is a basic lack of knowledge, and the resources to acquire that knowledge, concerning the full extent of the archaeological database. These are mostly upland regions, often with monuments that survive to a much greater extent than in areas with more active cultivation histories. In the absence of comprehensive Sites and Monuments Records, or even adequate archaeological officers to compile them, the procedures of monitoring afforestation and advising the Forestry Commission are almost impossible to carry out effectively.

The new Community Forests of lowland England will presumably pose less of a problem for archaeology as they are to be established in areas which for the most part already have comprehensive SMR's and adequate numbers of 'archaeological curators' in local authority planning departments.

Archaeology and Agricultural Policy

All changes in agricultural land-use have archaeological implications. The introduction of less intensive exploitation will usually mean less destruction of archaeological remains, whilst new drainage and clearance, and new or deeper ploughing will almost always result in increased, and potentially disastrous damage.

New and altered agricultural policy, whether nationally, or EEC - derived therefore has implications for archaeology, even if the subject itself is not addressed by the policy literature. Happily recent schemes such as 'Set-aside' and 'Beef and Sheep Extensification' will for the most part result in less archaeological impact, but this is not an argument for reduced concern in such areas. Farm and Conservation Grant Schemes, by providing grants for the repair and reinstatement of traditional farm buildings, encourage the retention of existing historic structures in the rural landscape, when they may otherwise be too expensive to maintain and be left to decay to the point of collapse or necessary demolition. Other schemes, however, such as Farm Woodland Schemes and Farm Diversification Schemes, can have all the destructive potential for the historic environment of any other area development. On the whole MAFF (or the relevant national/regional Office) has no specific archaeological policies for these schemes, and it is up to the archaeological advisors of the relevant LPA to publicise and moderate potentially destructive changes where possible. As planning legislation is very limited in its application to agricultural practices, this is often a difficult task.

On a brighter note, MAFF has recently been working in partnership with English Heritage to provide guidance for farmers on limiting damage to archaeological remains. The booklet *Farming Historic Landscapes and Peoples* states

"Not everything from the past can or should be conserved, but we do need to save enough for our children to study and learn from.

Please use your influence to conserve what is left for future generations" (MAFF/English Heritage 1991).

The language may not be exactly how an archaeologist would like it phrased, but the positive intention towards preservation is clear.

The Historic Parks and Gardens Register

One of the more prominent growth areas in British field archaeology in recent years has been the emergence of the sub-discipline of 'garden archaeology'. This has occurred as part of a more general increase in the awareness of the importance of historic parks and gardens, amongst individuals and organisations representing the broad spread of 'conservation disciplines'.

English Heritage acknowledged these developments through the establishment of a 'Register of parks and gardens of special historic interest in England' which was assembled between 1984 and 1988. This has been updated and computerised more recently, and individual additions are made to the register as necessary.

As with listed buildings, parks and gardens on the register are graded I, II* and II. Unlike the listing process, however, the register has no statutory basis and thus no *direct* protection is afforded to those parks and gardens on the list. Instead it is the intention of English Heritage that by placing parks and gardens on the register, attention will be drawn to them and thus owners, local authorities and developers will ensure that they are "safeguarded in any plans for development." (David Jacques, *Cons. Bull.* 13, Feb. 1991). Jacques also points out that "in several public enquiries it has been established that the historic interest of a park or garden is a material planning consideration" (*op cit*). Furthermore, in guidance documents published by the DoE and DoT advice is given that explicitly recommends the avoidance of historic parks and gardens when planning developments.

Thus, if sympathetic policies relating to historic parks and gardens are written into revisions of local plans, and if developers and government departments identify their presence and alter development proposals accordingly, then parks and gardens on the register are afforded due consideration and protection. The whole process does however rely on sympathetic treatment, and where major destruction is not avoided by a developer and the local planning authority allows the work to proceed, the only recourse for those wishing to protect the 'listed' area, is a public enquiry.

Jacque's paper in *Conservation Bulletin* 13 (*op cit.*) admits that the system does not always prove satisfactory, identifying how historic landscape can be quickly eroded by numerous small decisions which lie outside normal planning control, particularly those relating to agricultural exploitation. His concluding remarks which, although not *de facto* English Heritage policy, can be taken to in general indicate the corporate approach, state that:

> "In the end, the quality of each garden or park depends upon the owner's enthusiasm and care, and it is thus vital for them to appreciate the value of what they possess, and to know how to

> look after it. English Heritage seeks to persuade owners to take an active interest and encourages them by providing information, and, resources permitting, by assisting schemes of repair through grants. The work of other agencies, such as the Countryside Commission and the Forestry Commission, in guiding the evolution of the landscape is of vital importance too". (Jacques, *op cit.*).

Structures within gardens can be listed as 'Listed Buildings'. Furthermore parks and gardens could theoretically be scheduled as ancient monuments, although there are good reasons why this has not so far been done; not the least of which is the fundamental 'evolving' nature of gardens which is at odds with the 'fossilisation' concept of scheduling.

Legislation for Statutory Undertakers

Statutory undertakers have long had heritage conservation and archaeological responsibilities. Some of the privatisation legislation of the last few years has resulted in a stricter definition of these responsibilities.

The Water Act

In particular the *Water Act 1989* imposes duties on the water companies and the NRA which require them to 'have regard for the desirability of protecting and conserving buildings (including structures), sites and objects of archaeological, architectural and historic interest,' for the protection of their setting and amenity value, and the maintenance of public access (Part 1, Para 8(1)).

The Water Act also provides for the extension of such protection to land sold by the water companies and the National Rivers Authority (NRA), through management agreements or covenants governing future land use and access, or encouraging good conservation practice. These procedures only apply to the disposal of designated land such as that within National Parks, Areas of Outstanding Natural Beauty, and Sites of Special Scientific Interest. It is often these areas that possess the richest archaeological information, but it would perhaps be more encouraging if such schemes could also be applied to Sites of Archaeological Interest, as defined in the *General Development Order 1988*.

The Electricity Act

Environmental and archaeological protection under the *Electricity Act 1989* rests ultimately with the Secretary of State, but there is provision for such responsibilities to be passed on to individual companies as conditions of their operating licences. Schedule 9 of the Act does require licence holders to 'have regard to the desirability of...protecting sites, buildings (including structures) and objects of architectural, historic or archaeological interest'. They are also required to provide a statement outlining how these duties will be fulfilled. The major national power companies have already submitted outline environmental policy and their full Schedule 9 statements are expected to be similar to the Water Act Code. They will undoubtedly act as a model for similar documents from smaller companies.

Burials and Burial Grounds Legislation

The laws relating to interment, protection and exhumation of human remains are complex, furthermore they are apparently different in each part of the United Kingdom. English Law is that which is addressed below. The situation in Northern Ireland and the Channel Islands is not discussed, nor is Scottish law considered, although it is perhaps worth pointing out that in Scotland there is no legal differentiation between a generally accepted 'burial place' and any other location where bodies have been left or found.

Under Section 25 of the *Burial Act 1857*, it is a criminal offence to remove human remains from a place of burial without a licence. These are available from the Home Office once certain information has been provided, and a £10 fee paid. The maximum fine for the unlicensed removal of human remains will shortly be increased to £200.

The usual procedure on discovery of human remains is to contact the police and, if the discovery is made by building contractors rather than archaeologists, a local archaeological body is also required. The archaeologists will then be able to advise on the date of the burial which, if less than fifty years old, will necessitate the involvement of the coroner. If older than fifty years, then a Section 25 licence will allow its removal.

The *Disused Burial Grounds Acts of 1884 and 1981* provide protection for human remains within former burial grounds under threat of development. Section 2(1) of the 1981 Act provides that no building shall be erected upon a disused burial ground unless human remains have been removed and cremated or re-interred in accordance with the provisions of the Schedule to the Act.

The Museum of London Act

The Museum of London possesses its own act of parliament (The

Museum of London Act 1986), which is mostly concerned with the composition and functions of the board of governors, and the sources of establishment funding. This act replaced provisions in the Local Government Act 1985, which in turn replaced the original Museum of London Act (1965). These changes were necessitated by the abolition of the GLC, which up until 1985 supplied one third of the governors of the Museum and one third of its establishment costs. The 1986 act states that the board is empowered to provide archaeological services and to undertake archaeological research in Greater London and the surrounding region. Such work is not, however, classified under the Museum's statutory functions and thus, other than a very few posts, central funding for archaeological staff is limited.

Legislation in Maritime Archaeology

Maritime archaeology is subject to two pieces of legislation, the *Protection of Wrecks Act 1973*, and the *Merchant Shipping Act 1894*.

The Protection of Wrecks Act 1973

The objective of this piece of legislation is defined by government as:

"to ensure that wrecks of historical, archaeological or artistic importance in United Kingdom territorial waters are protected from unauthorised interference and that only competent and properly equipped people survey and excavate such sites". (DoT, Historic Wrecks Guidance Note 1986, 2.).

The 1973 Act empowers the Secretary of State for Transport (now Heritage) to make designation orders which identify the site of the wrecked vessel and the extent of the 'restricted area' around it. Within this area it is an offence to carry out activities which can be broadly defined as tampering with, damaging, or removing any part of the wrecked vessel or anything contained in it. It is also an offence to carry out any diving or salvage operations, or deposit anything which will obliterate or obstruct access to the site, or damage the wreck. Before making a designation order the Secretary of State is normally required to consult 'appropriate persons', which usually means the Advisory Committee on Historic Wreck Sites (a body comprising archaeologists, museums staff and divers as well as civil servants). Once designated, a wreck is marked with a buoy, and relevant notice is made on Admiralty charts. If organisations wish to excavate or survey a designated wreck an application for a licence can be made. Such applications are considered by the Advisory Committee, who make recommendations to the Secretary of State.

The 1973 Act is undoubtedly a piece of legislation that works, but only in the few instances when it has been applied. There are at present only 35 designated wrecks, in approximately 66,660sq miles of territorial waters (twelve miles from coast). Furthermore almost all of these sites are off the south coast of England, with none between Shetland and the Thames Estuary in the east, and only six between the Hebrides and Lands End in the west. The reasons for such a woefully small number of designations are twofold. Firstly, the Advisory Committee only advises on designations that are presented to it. Thus many wrecks worthy of preservation, but without an active supporting body, may not come to the attention of the committee. Secondly, the Department of National Heritage's budget for the inspection of designated wrecks and for research into new designations is at present only about £150,00 per annum. Until recently most of this money has been awarded to the University of St. Andrews Archaeological Diving Unit (ADU) which, although strictly only a tendering body, is well recognised for its expertise in the inspection of designated sites and the provision of advice on the assessment of proposals for designation. The ADU, and any other bodies that successfully tender for this money, represent the only organisations with funding from central government that deal with the problems of nautical archaeology in this country. Thus funds are not available for large scale mapping of potential designation sites, nor is there much scope for the investigation of new or old discoveries which may be being looted.

'Wreck Material', The Merchant Shipping Act 1894

The second piece of relevant legislation is the 1894 Merchant Shipping Act, Part IX of which deals with 'wreck material'. All finds from designated sites are classified as 'wreck material' and must be delivered to the 'Receiver of Wreck', which usually means the local customs officer. If the owner of the material cannot be identified (very likely in the case of archaeological finds), then the 'Receiver of Wreck' is empowered to sell or dispose of the material. The law states that the proceeds from disposal go to the Crown, after deduction of VAT and commission, although it is now common practice for the items to be disposed of in such a way that the finder receives a reasonable amount. In this way it is hoped that disclosure is encouraged.

That finds from historic wrecks, as recognised important sites, are disposed of under a nineteenth century law designed to deal with sinkings as they occur is undeniably a cause for concern. The legislation as it stands is also an encouragement to recover and sell finds, whether to finance further excavations (as with the case of HMS Invincible, Sheldon 1988), or purely for profit. There is a strong case for new legislation that treats such material in the manner it deserves. However, in the absence of governmental support for real land-based portable antiquities legislation, it is doubtful whether any maritime equivalent is likely in the near future.

'Heritage at Sea'

In 1989 the Joint Nautical Archaeology Policy Committee, which consists of representatives from the CBA, IFA, The National Maritime Museum and the Nautical Archaeology Society, submitted to government a paper (*Heritage at Sea*) outlining problems with the provisions, both monetary and legislative, for maritime archaeology in Britain. Their proposals included recommendations for new legislation specifically drafted for the protection of underwater sites and for much more responsibility, on behalf of government and its agencies, for the protection of marine archaeology. This would include a national inventory of underwater archaeological sites and the creation of a maritime heritage protection agency. Furthermore, it pressed for the implementation of policies encouraging commercial seabed operators to carry out archaeological implication surveys, and to contribute to the cost of any necessary archaeological works.

Since then the governmental environment white paper 'This Common Inheritance' (Sept 1990) stated the intention to transfer responsibility for Historic Wrecks from the DTP to the DoE, but now in fact the Heritage Ministry, and also stated that the National Maritime Museum would be brought into discussions regarding Historic Wrecks where appropriate. Both of these moves have distinct advantages for the management of the situation as it stands, but neither will necessarily result in more money to be spent on designations and monitoring, which is what is really required so long as the basic legislation remains unaltered. Furthermore, the possibility that the small sum of money currently available will be divided up amongst more than one successful tendering body, exacerbates an already difficult situation.

Most recently a detailed governmental response to *Heritage at Sea* has been provided which indicates that the present legislation is under review, but that no major change is foreseen in the near future. The government also states that it does not see a need for the setting up of a new maritime heritage protection agency. The Royal Commissions have, however, been 'invited' to start work on preparing central records of historic wrecks, and the RCHME has already initiated such a scheme. Another promising recent development, partly in response to *Heritage at Sea*, is the recently drafted *Code of Conduct for Seabed Operators*, which was compiled by the Joint Nautical Archaeological Policy Committee. The basis of this document, as with land-based archaeological planning guidance, is that early contact between developers and archaeologists is the key to sympathetic 'development' schemes.

All in all the 'picture' for Maritime Archaeology looks much better now than it did even only a couple of years ago. However, Government policy still shies away from real protective measures brought about through new legislation, a state of affairs not very different from that witnessed on land.

The Department of National Heritage

One of the most significant recent developments in governmental attitude to the protection of the physical remains of the past was the creation in 1992 of the Department of National Heritage and appointment of a minister for 'Heritage'. That this post's remit encompassed aspects of leisure, the arts and sport as well might not have satisfied all those who had campaigned for many years to ensure that 'heritage' matters had a real voice in government, but it should still have been a useful step forward. Unfortunately the new department's responsibilities do not encompass all areas that influence the fate of archaeological and historic remains and thus it seems that a great opportunity to create once and for all a single strong voice for 'Heritage' in government in England has indeed been missed.

The Department of National Heritage's first document was a joint circular with the DoE, identifying the new department's conservation responsibilities (*Department of the Environment (20/92) and Department of National Heritage (1/92) Joint Circular, Responsibilities for Conservation Policy and Casework*). The document states that:

"Policy responsibility for archaeology and the conservation of the built environment now rests with the Secretary of State for national Heritage" (para. 2). It then goes on immediately to explain:

"To ensure that the necessary co-ordination of planning and conservation policy is maintained, formal jurisdiction on certain types of heritage casework remains with the Secretary of State for the Environment" (para. 3).

The casework transferred to the DNH includes scheduling and scheduled monument consents, listing, repairs notices, urgent works notices and associated land acquisition. It does not, however, include listed building and conservation area consents and appeals against 'call - in' decisions on listed buildings, which remain the responsibility of the DoE, presumably because they are perceived as forming part of wider planning legislation considerations. There seems to be no concern in government circles that one department is responsible for deciding which buildings are important enough to be listed, whilst another department considers which developments affecting listed buildings are acceptable or unacceptable.

With regard to historic wrecks the situation is no clearer, with the Department of National Heritage responsible for designations, but the Department of Transport still apparently regulating wreck material. The documentation on this subject states the DNH remit as;

"responsibility for the protection of wrecks (section 1 of the protection of Wrecks Act 1973), and for nautical archaeology generally." (*op. cit.*)

The latter half of this statement does not explain matters satisfactorily. Despite these obvious problems the creation of the Department of National Heritage must be seen as a step forward. It is to be hoped that in time its roles will be better defined and it will become more all-encompassing where 'heritage matters' are concerned. It might best be seen as a new gravitational object, that will eventually pull together the various strands of heritage-related legislation into one defined 'orbit'.

The powers of the department of National Heritage do not, of course, extend into Scotland, Wales and Northern Ireland, responsibility in most 'Heritage' matters outside of England remains with the Scottish and Welsh Offices and the DoE (Northern Ireland).

Part 2 Archaeology and the Planning Process

Whilst the *Ancient Monuments and Archaeological Areas Act 1979* is undoubtedly comprehensive in its consideration of SAMs and AAIs, it is precisely this feature of the act, that it is only concerned with such designated sites and urban landscapes and not with archaeological remains in general, that renders it useless in most cases of threat to the archaeological heritage.

Developments that happen to threaten archaeological remains will, however, often be subject to planning law. Although recently consolidated (*Town and Country Planning Act 1990*), general planning legislation does not consider archaeological remains specifically. However, in cases where the execution of the works proposed in a planning application would undoubtedly damage known (or presumed) archaeological material, there are procedures by which the planning authority can require the developer to pay due regard to the archaeology. This is through the use of 'conditions' which can be imposed upon the relevant application and which allow development to proceed only if the condition is satisfied. A DoE and Welsh Office circular on the use of planning conditions cites the presence of areas of possible archaeological interest as an acceptable basis for a condition, enabling the 'monument' to be protected, or ensuring that archaeologists are allowed access during the course of; "carrying out the permitted works" *(DoE & Welsh Office Joint Circular 1/85*).

The 1990 Town and Country Planning legislation defines two things which a planning authority must have regard to when determining planning applications, these being the relevant Development Plan (i.e. Structure Plans and Local Plans) and "any other material consideration". Archaeology was first defined as a material consideration by Lord Denning in an Appeal Court ruling in the mid 1970s, and this position was reaffirmed in DoE Guidance note 8/87, and most recently in PPG16 (1990).

Structure and local plans which "provide the necessary framework for development control and the co-ordination and direction of development" (*DoE & Welsh Office Joint Circular 22/84*) may also protect archaeology at the local level through making recommendations as to the type of developments that will be acceptable within specifically-defined restraint areas, the presence of historic and archaeological remains being one basis on which such restraint maps are drawn up.

This system, based around planning conditions, can work when approached in a positive manner by all bodies concerned. To aid in this a number of publications have been produced which represent explicit guidelines for all parties involved, be they developers, planners, curators or contracting archaeologists.

The CBI Code for Mineral Operators

The first of these to be published was the *CBI Archaeological Investigations Code of Practice for Mineral Operators.* Originally appearing in 1982, this document has recently been extensively updated and republished (April 1991), with an introductory welcoming endorsement by the Under Secretary of State for the Environment. The code

"sets out recommended procedures and standards for consultation and co-operation between mineral operators, planners and archaeologists... The original code was produced in response to the *Ancient Monuments and Archaeological Areas Act 1979* and gave mineral operators exemption from certain sections of the act in exchange for adherence to the code."

The code was rewritten to take account of changes in planning legislation and the organisation and funding of archaeology. The amended code has been agreed to by the DoE, the Welsh Office, English Heritage and the Association of County Archaeological Officers (who actually drafted it), and was written in consultation with the Association of County Councils (ACC) and the Association of Metropolitan Authorities (AMA). The code stresses the need for all relevant parties to identify the likely presence of archaeological sites, which may be affected by the development, as early as possible, specifically indicating that developers should consult the relevant SMR and archaeological body (usually the County Archaeologist) and allow the latter access to the site for inspection. It also states that there may be a need for an archaeological evaluation before a fully informed planning application can be made, and that this must be executed to a specification which is acceptable to the mineral planning authority and which should be carried out by a "qualified archaeological contractor" (para. 2.5, p.5). On the basis of all such information the planning application would then include "outline proposals necessary to accommodate any significant archaeological interests" (para. 2.7, p.6).

The guidelines discuss the various outcomes that are possible from the planning decision, and provide a model statement where development is subject to an archaeologically-derived planning condition.

"No development shall take place within the area indicated (this could be the area of archaeological interest) until the applicant has secured the implementation of a programme of archaeological work in accordance with a written scheme of investigation which has been submitted by the applicant and approved by the mineral planning authority" (para. 2.10, p.7).

This model statement is intended to render unnecessary legal agreements between developers and mineral planning authorities, regarding archaeological work. As regards the funding of those archaeological works that are deemed necessary, the code states...

"The CBI supports the practice of mineral operators offering financial or practical assistance to archaeological excavations to implement the scheme..." (para. 2.11, p.8)

This is in line with any broad 'polluter pays' principle, but without any explicit legal framework for such a process, the enforcement of the code in general, and the matter of funding in particular, rests with the mineral planning authority in question and the nature of the condition they enforce.

The BADLG Code of Practice

The British Archaeologists and Developers Liaison Group (BADLG) Code of Practice was originally published in 1986, but has been republished twice since (1988 and 1991). This code, endorsed by all relevant bodies, aims to achieve; "a realistic understanding between archaeologists and developers...on a voluntary basis" (BADLG 1991). To this end it sets out two codes, one for archaeologists, and one for developers, adherence to which will theoretically smooth the way for understanding and co-operation during the negotiation and execution of archaeological works as part of the development process. The code, like the CBI code, stresses the need for all parties to become aware of their obligations and roles early on in the process, for information concerning all aspects of work undertaken by all parties to be freely distributed between parties, for publicity and educational factors to be properly managed, and for proper consideration to be given to longer term aspects of the works, such as archiving, publication and display. There is no doubt that the code can be of great benefit when used properly, however, the only developers represented in the Liaison Group are those that are members of the British Property Federation (BPF). Many developers are not members of the BPF, and no information is available regarding the identity of members so archaeologists don't actually know which developers might be held to the code. Finally, the code is only voluntary, and there is little that can be done to persuade developers to adhere to it, regardless of whether they are BPF members or not.

Planning Policy Guidance 16, Archaeology and Planning (PPG16)

The most recent document of note in relation to its recommendations on the protection of archaeology through the planning process is the DoE paper *Planning Policy Guidance 16, Archaeology and Planning (PPG16).* This paper specifically addresses the problem of dealing with archaeology within extant planning law, and replaces previous government guidance notes such as the joint DoE and Welsh Office circulars already discussed (22/84 & 1/85) and DoE circular 8/87 (itself a re-statement of much earlier guidance, i.e.. 23/77). PPG16 only applies in England, however, and it is only very recently (early 1992) that a comparable document for Wales has been published.

PPG16 sets out with explicit aims of stating:

"the Secretary of State's *(Environment)* policy on archaeological remains on land, and how they should be preserved or recorded" (PPG16, Para.1, Nov. 1990).

The thrust of this policy (for England only) is that the needs of archaeology and development can indeed be reconciled, and particularly that early consultation, by developers, with the planning authority can greatly reduce any potential conflict. Where a development proposal may damage archaeology, attempts can be made to plan the development around the relevant sensitive areas, preserving them *in situ.*

If necessary the developer may wish to employ an archaeological consultant to determine the presence, extent and value of such features that may exist. Primary information can of course be obtained from the local SMR, County Archaeologist, and possibly English Heritage or Cadw under the Welsh guidance note.

Through PPG16 the DoE make great efforts to highlight 'Field Evaluation' as a key stage in the consideration of Archaeology during development. By field evaluation they mean a normally "rapid and inexpensive operation, involving ground survey and small scale trenching" (PPG16, para 21). This method of data gathering is already familiar to English field units, and despite its obviously important role in management of the archaeological heritage, it cannot be said to be always the most intellectually satisfying area of archaeological fieldwork. However, evaluation is a vital stage in the procedure recommended in PPG16 and in support of the use of evaluations this document states "it is reasonable for the planning authority to request the prospective developer to arrange for an archaeological field evaluation to be carried out before any decision on the planning application is taken" (*op cit.*). If all such measures do not result in development that avoids, or takes account of, known or supposed archaeological remains, then the alternative will usually mean some form of excavation.

The text of PPG16 is at great pains to indicate that preservation ***in situ*** is usually regarded as the best alternative. Also, Paragraph 25 directly states that:

"Planning authorities should not include in their development plans any policies requiring developers to finance archaeological works in return for the grant of planning permission..." but that where preservation ***in situ*** is not justified "and that development resulting in the destruction of the archaeological remains should proceed, it would be entirely reasonable for the planning authority to satisfy itself before granting planning permission, that the developer has made appropriate and satisfactory provision for the excavation and recording of the remains" (DoE, Nov. 1990, para. 25). If the planning authority is not satisfied that adequate steps have been taken it can "secure excavation by imposing conditions" (*ibid.*).

This therefore is how government policy sees the use of the planning constraint in the protection of archaeological remains. If adequate consultation is sought at an early stage in development plans, the need for a planning condition will generally be avoided. Such an approach, although undoubtedly laudable does require the planning authority to be fully sympathetic to the needs of archaeology. Unfortunately this is not always the case, and instances may well arise where local economics dictate that the pursuit of lucrative developments, theoretically beneficial for the community as a whole, might well result in a less than sympathetic ear on the part of the planning authority for the needs of the archaeology under threat. In such a situation no mechanism exists for adequate protection of archaeological remains.

Despite the good intentions that many planning authorities show towards archaeology, the fact remains that none of their powers that relate to the curation of the archaeological heritage are mandatory. Outside scheduled ancient monuments and designated AAIs, there is no legal requirement for planning constraints to be applied, whatever the perceived value of the archaeological remains. Thus, whenever a planning body deems other considerations relating to the development to be more important, a condition may not be applied and the archaeology can be destroyed without record. Furthermore, unless the condition specifically states that the developing body either avoids destroying the archaeological material or funds *all* necessary archaeological work, then it is possible that there will not be sufficient funds made available to complete and publish the results of the investigation. In such a situation it may be possible to request funding from the relevant national heritage organisation, but this is not an ideal method of maintaining adequate protection for the nation's archaeology.

General Discussion

It is a generally recognised fact that many developments in many parts of the country could not support the complete excavation of complex archaeological remains, plus all the necessary specialist work, archiving and publication. Furthermore any attempts to enforce legislation designed to impose such measures in a wholesale fashion would lead to confrontation with the development industry. The imposition of such 'sledgehammer' legislation would almost certainly prejudice the smaller developments in less economically buoyant areas as well as developments by non-profit making organisations and small landowners. Often it is precisely in those areas of the country where archaeological coverage is poorest, and where research goals are most pressing that development might be curtailed to the greatest extent by over-vigorous protection policies. But, as archaeologists, we are bound to protect the physical remains of the past, for if *we* don't, then no one else will. It is, however, our duty to society to balance this against the legitimate needs of our modern communities.

So, does the present system of voluntary action by planning authorities and gentle persuasion of development bodies work well enough? The answer to this question is one which will vary according to which region or county is being discussed, and which developer and which archaeological contractor are involved. The main dictating factor is, purely and simply, in which way, and to what extent, the voluntary codes are applied. The 'rogue' variables in the equation are not the 'codes', they are those who interpret the codes and make the decisions, those who create the briefs and specifications for the archaeological work that is to be required. The developers are not specialists in these matters, they will generally follow where led, so long as the price is right. The archaeological body should be working to a brief which is sufficiently tightly drawn to exclude the possibility of substandard tenders being submitted and accepted and the execution of which is monitored. It is the county archaeological officers, and their equivalents, who in general advise the planning authorities and construct such briefs, and the planning authorities who incorporate these proposals into consents and constraints. As Simon Buteux stated recently (1991), this major part of the archaeological planning process is the one area that is totally unmonitored. It is not the intention of this text to insult archaeological curators, as in general they execute the tasks necessary to satisfy the archaeology and planning guidance literature as well as is humanly possible. Concern must however be expressed where only one or two officers are making all the decisions regarding the quality and context of archaeological specifications for a whole county. Lack of resources to employ more staff, or increase data collection and field visits, is the fundamental problem here. If County Council officers are to be the 'curators', then the County Councils need to be able to provide enough resources to fund teams with the requisite knowledge to cover the impact of development on the archaeology of all periods, in all parts of the relevant county. It is doubtful whether this is the present state of affairs in many counties.

Beyond the reach of PPG16: Destructive processes not requiring planning permission.

Only part of our archaeological heritage can, when threatened, be dealt with through planning law, or planning agreements. A large portion of our archaeology is threatened from what can be termed 'landuse changes'. These, in many instances, are not subject to legislation that can be used to protect or preserve what is being lost. Such problems apply almost exclusively to the rural regions, and the result is woefully inadequate protection for what are often our most complete relict landscapes. The archaeological community has been aware of the impact that modern agricultural methods and increased afforestation can make in eroding our archaeological resource for several decades. These were amongst the primary concerns voiced in literature that characterised the setting up of RESCUE itself; e.g. the initial 1971 memorandum to the DoE (reprinted in Fowler 1972). Since then these problems have been periodically raised within archaeology, but the success of archaeologists in bringing such matters to public and governmental attention has been very variable. One major development has been the growth in concern for the preservation of cultural/historical landscapes alongside natural ones, on the part of the statutory countryside bodies (the Countryside Stewardship scheme being a good recent example of this). Furthermore the Forestry Commission's recent "generally sympathetic attitude" (Prehist. Soc. 1988, 3) towards the preservation of the cultural heritage has only come about since the adoption of more environmentally enlightened procedures by this body. This may indeed suggest that major successes in protecting our diminishing rural archaeological resource have usually only come about when the erosion of archaeology has been highlighted as part of wider environmental concerns. It is not just in the uplands, however, that great losses of archaeological information (and our cultural heritage) are occurring. Throughout lowland Britain our remaining prehistoric sites and boundaries are still disappearing, whilst the drying out of wetlands, and the grave consequences for some of our best preserved archaeology that this brings, is an issue that never recedes in importance.

In 1988 the Prehistoric Society published a paper entitled 'Saving Our Prehistoric Heritage' which outlined the scale of these continuing threats, specifically with regard to prehistoric landscapes, but in reality of relevance to the protection of monuments of all ages. This document warned of the imminent further destruction of rural landscapes through land use changes initiated by European Community agricultural policy. The paper suggested that the incorporation of archaeological awareness in the development of agricultural set-aside policy could be very beneficial to the protection of our remaining rural archaeology, but that the absence of such considerations would see a very rapid acceleration of destruction as the pace of land use change quickened.

Until recently little headway had been made in the fight to get these losses recognised by government, or its agents. 1990 saw, however, the publication of the government white paper on the environment *This Common Inheritance*, which has spurred English Heritage, and hopefully the other national heritage bodies, into action as regards compiling lists of landscapes of historic importance. A recent English Heritage policy statement outlined the general approach being adopted in England. This will result in a register which;

"could provide a non-statutory guide for owners, local authorities and others with an interest in countryside management. A major objective would be to ensure that nationally important landscapes of historic interest are identified, so that they can be accorded appropriate special treatment. At the same time, since a sense of place is very much a local matter, local perspectives and the value attached to the familiar and the cherished, and to locally important landscapes, should also be recognised and supported" (*Cons. Bull.* 14, June 1991).

Whether this will result in a register with two classes of landscape, of local and national importance is, at present, uncertain. It is obvious, however, that there is no intention on the part of government, nor so far any call from the national heritage bodies, to provide real legislative protection for registered landscapes. The pivotal statement in the English Heritage text is perhaps one identifying the 'way forward' as "through partnership, rather than restriction" (*op. cit.*), which sounds rather as if it has been culled straight from the 'white paper'. The English Heritage statement is at pains to state that the means of conservation already exist "in the wide range of legislative instruments, planning controls and grant schemes which are available" (*op. cit.*). Surely, if this were the case, then there would in fact be no need to create a historic landscapes register? Despite this, any initiative of this type has got to be welcome, if only to indicate that the conservation of historic landscapes is now an acknowledged concern on the governmental agenda. Whether the list of designations is successful in any conservation sense, or whether the result is another truncated and half-forgotten edifice, as with the AAIs, remains to be seen.

English Heritage's recent consultation paper *Register of Landscapes of Historic Importance* (EH, October 1991) is not very difficult in approach to the initial statement in *Consultation Bulletin* 14. An introductory outline of topics considered includes the statement "these policies must recognise the inevitability of change, and the need for the thoughtful direction and management of necessary changes in order to avoid sterile fossilisation". (English Heritage, October 1991). Such aims are laudable, but the same document suggests that this might be achieved solely through the creation of an agreed methodology for identifying and assessing the 'historic environment' rather than through the creation of a separate list or register. It is therefore, already apparent that at least one national heritage body is questioning the fundamental concept of a need for a 'historic landscapes register'. If this is in reality the way we are heading, then the onus is on professional archaeologists within local authorities to do what they can to protect their local historic landscapes through the alternatives of introducing landscape preservation concepts into the relevant local development plans. The criteria for inclusion of a 'historic landscape' into such documentation would presumably still derive from whatever methodology the relevant national heritage body had in the meantime deemed appropriate.

General Conclusions

The reader who has progressed this far will undoubtedly agree that legislation dealing with archaeological matters in the United Kingdom is incomplete and patchy in its coverage. The large number of government-derived documents that have been briefly considered in these pages bear witness to the fact that an archaeological provision is usually an afterthought rather than a central consideration in both governmental guidance and statutory law. Furthermore in some instances, treasure trove law being a good example, the legislation is hopelessly antiquated and inadequate for the modern task to which it has to be applied.

Since the 1979 Act, and more recently and perhaps more importantly since the arrival of PPG16, the provision for the protection of archaeology in law and through the planning process has become very much better. This does not mean, however, that Britain's Archaeology is now safe. Far from it in fact. The pressures of the last years of the twentieth century on the historic fabric of the country are greater than they have ever been. Even in times of economic stagnation we are still losing too many irreplaceable pieces of our past and we are doing ourselves a disservice if we claim otherwise.

The fact that we now have a Department for National Heritage in central government does provide some indication that the message that the past needs proper protection is getting through to those with the power to do something about it. There is, of course, still a long way to go. As I write I am aware that a 'Hedgerows' Bill has been approved by Government and thus before long we will have the resultant Act. From the text of the Bill it seems that at last a piece of legislation is being drafted that recognises the dual historical AND natural-environmental importance of part of our rural landscape. The environmental lobby, rather than archaeologists, may well have been the most influential voice in the successful passage of this piece of legislation, but it is still a very important step towards a wider perspective on landscape curation and may represent a watershed in Governmental thinking.

RESCUE has been working for many years to draw attention to the gaps in archaeological protection provided by legislation in the UK. Efforts have been directed towards highlighting a number of specific and glaring inadequacies, as well as the consideration of a more general lack of understanding and awareness of the need to protect the physical remains of the past. In all such work RESCUE does, however, need support and it is the author's firm belief that by joining and/or working with RESCUE you can help to protect our past.

Bibliography

The bibliography has not been ordered in the conventional alphabetical fashion, but instead on a thematic basis that takes account of the variety of source types.

A) Current United Kingdom legislation referred to in the text.

Burial Act 1857.
Disused Burial Grounds Act 1884.
Merchant Shipping Act 1894.
Ancient Monuments (Northern Ireland) Act 1925.
The Forestry Act 1967.
Countryside Act 1968..
Protection of Wrecks Act 1973..
Ancient Monuments and Archaeological Areas Act 1979.
Disused Burial Grounds Act 1981.
The Ancient Monuments (Class Consents) Order 1981.
Wildlife and Countryside Act 1981.
National Heritage Act 1983.
Agriculture Act 1986.
Museum of London Act 1986.
Town and Country Planning (Assessment of Environmental Effects) Regulations 1988.
Town and Country Planning General Development Order 1988.
Electricity Act 1989.
Water Act 1989.
Planning (Listed Buildings and Conservation Areas) Act 1990.
Town and Country Planning Act 1990.
The Planning (Listed Building and Conservation Areas) Regulations 1990 (Stat. Inst. 1519)
Planning and Compensation Act 1991.

B) Other Government documents and publications referred to in the text.

Memorandum on Structure and Local Plans, Department of the Environment (22/84) and Welsh Office (43/84) Joint Circular, 7th September 1984. (Now replaced by the new edition of PPG12).
The use of conditions in planning permissions, Department of the Environment (1/85) and Welsh Office (1/85) Joint Circular, 7th January 1985.
Historic Wrecks Guidance Note, Department of Transport Marine Directorate, December 1986.
Historic Buildings and Conservation Areas - Policy and Procedures, DoE Circular 8/87.
Environmental Assessment, DoE (15/88) and Welsh Office (23/88) Joint Circular 12th July 1988.
This Common Inheritance: Britain's Environmental Strategy,

Governmental White Paper, September 1990, HMSO.
Planning Policy Guidance Note 16: Archaeology and Planning (PPG16), Department of the Environment, November 1990.
Consultation Paper - Ancient Monuments, Department of the Environment Heritage Division, April 1990.
Responsibilities for Conservation Policy and Casework, Department of the Environment (20/92) and Department of National Heritage (1/92) Joint Circular.

C) Portable antiquities documents.

Convention on the means of prohibiting and preventing the illicit import, export and transfer of ownership of cultural property, UNESCO, 14th November 1970.
Treasure Trove: Law Reform Issues, Law Commission, September 1987.
Draft version of *A Bill Intituled* for a portable antiquities act, 10th December 1990.

D) Other publications referenced in the text.

BADLG, 1991, *The British Archaeologists and Developers Liaison Group Code of Practice.*
Buteux S., 1991, 'Competition in Archaeology: A Pragmatic Approach', in H. Swain (ed.) *Competitive Tendering in Archaeology* 13-20, SCAUM and RESCUE.
CBA, 1992, 'Government Questioned on Illicit Traffic in Antiquities', *British Archaeological News* Vol 7, No 2, 16.
CBI, 1991, *Archaeological Investigations Code of Practice for Mineral Operators,* Confederation of British Industry.
Countryside Commission, 1987, *The National Park Authority.*
Countryside Commission, 1991, *An Agenda For the Countryside.*
Countryside Commission, March 1991, *Fit for the Future, Report of the National Parks Review Committee.*
English Heritage, 1991, 'The Historic Landscape: An English Heritage Policy Statement', *Conservation Bulletin* **14**, (June 1991), 4-5.
English Heritage, October 1991 *'Register of Landscapes of Historic Importance: A Consultation Paper.'*
Fairclough G., 1990, 'Countryside Legislation and Statutory Codes of Practice', *Conservation Bulletin* **11**, June 1990, 12-13.
Fowler, P.J., 1972, 'Field Archaeology in Future: The Crisis and the Challenge', in P.J. Fowler (ed.) *Archaeology and the Landscape* 96-126, John Baker.
Henig 1986, 'The Pirates and their Treasure, from field to Bond Street', in H.Mytum and K.Waugh *Rescue Archaeology ; What's Next, Proceedings of a RESCUE Conference held at the University of York, December 1986*

Jacques, David, 1991, 'Planning for Parks and Gardens', *Cons. Bulletin* 13, (Feb '91) 12-13.
Joint Nautical Archaeology Policy Committee, 1989, Heritage at Sea (republished in *British Archaeological News* vol. **4**, no. **3**, May 1989).
MAFF/English Heritage, 1991, *Farming Historic Landscapes and people,* leaflet.
Nature Conservancy Council, English Heritage, Cadw, Historic Scotland, April 1991, *Joint Statement on Archaeology and Nature Conservation Policy.*
Plouviez J., 1989, 'Icklingham, A National Disgrace?', *Rescue News* **49**, 1-2.
The Prehistoric Society, 1988, *Saving Our Prehistoric Heritage.*
Proudfoot, E.V.W., 1989 *Our Vanishing Heritage: Forestry and Archaeology* CSA Occasional Papers No. 2.
Scott M., 1989, 'Scheduled but Unprotected: Ancient Monuments at Risk', *Rescue News* **49**, 4.
Sheldon H., 1988, 'Crisis in Maritime Archaeology', *Rescue News* **45**, 1-2.
Shepherd, I., 1989, 'Archaeology, Forestry and Planning: A Planning Problem', in Proudfoot 1989.

